## DATE DUE

| 6-9-16 | | | |
|---|---|---|---|
| 4-6-17 | | | |
| | | | |
| | | | |
| | | | |
| | | | |
| | | | |
| | | | |
| | | | |
| | | | |
| | | | |
| | | | |
| | | | |

Demco

# THE FIFTIES

**Editors: William Duffy, Robert Bly**

Third Issue                                                              1959

---

| | |
|---|---:|
| SOME NEW AMERICAN POEMS | 2 |
|     JAMES WRIGHT | |
|     MARGARET SCHEININ | |
|     ROBERT BLY | |
|     JEROME ROTHENBERG | |
|     GEORGE KRESENKY | |
| SOME THOUGHTS ON LORCA AND RENÉ CHAR | 7 |
| POEMS OF PAUL CELAN | 10 |
| THE NECESSITY OF REJECTING A SHAKESPEARE SONNET | 20 |
| POEMS OF MIRKO TUMA | 22 |
| THE WORK OF DONALD HALL | 32 |
|             —CRUNK | |
| FOUR CITY POEMS | 47 |
|     LOUIS SIMPSON | |
|     DAVID IGNATOW | |
|     DENISE LEVERTOV | |
| A NOTE ON HYDROGEN BOMB TESTING | 51 |
| MADAME TUSSAUD'S WAX MUSEUM | 52 |
| THE OTHER NIGHT IN HEAVEN | 54 |
|             —DIANA TILLING | |
| AWARD OF THE BLUE TOAD | 57 |
| PAUL CELAN | 58 |
| MIRKO TUMA | 59 |
| AMERICAN CONTRIBUTORS | 60 |

---

THE FIFTIES is published quarterly by The Fifties, Briarwood Hill, Pine Island, Minnesota. Subscriptions $2.00 per year in the U.S. and Canada; foreign $2.50. Single copy $.50. Manuscripts will not be returned unless accompanied by stamped, self-addressed envelopes. Payment: $10.00 per page for poems and translations of poems; $7.50 per page for prose. Printed by The Kerryman Ltd., Tralee, Ireland. Copyright © 1959 by The Fifties.

Reprint by Hobart & William Smith College Press in Association with the Seneca Review, Geneva, New York 14456

REPRINT BY PERMISSION OF THE EDITOR

JAMES WRIGHT

## THE DREAM OF THE AMERICAN FRONTIER

On First Avenue,
Seattle,
The wharf slowly fills its dawn
With Asian sailors.

Old men
Have been shipped out of Chicago
In the dark.

Deacons and janitors are drowning
Sweetly, on the last beaches
Of bay rum and salvation,
A flop of graves.

I wish I were the owner
Of the sea.

MARGARET SCHEININ

## THE GATES PARTED

Inward and downward was the way,
Below the drench of living waters in the thick darkness
And at the farthest inwardness, at the heart,
There is fire, flameless and unconsumed and Siva.
The only way out was the way down with
Vervain, hellebore in hand or any growing thing.
And the dead with dry mouths cross
The black trenches for blood;
Against the darkness, the shape of a leaf unfolds,
Not the clashing of spears, the striking of shield on shield
Nor the bull-roarer and the buccina, but the shape
Of the leaf stretching itself from pain,
From the urgency of the strong stem.

The terror of the cataract, of waters going down.


ROBERT BLY

## POEM

The wild bull is bleeding on the mountain.
But it is green, dark green,
In the wild cave of the Virgin.

In the cave of the Mother of Joy
From a bed of hot coals
The odor of rosemary and thyme is rising.

When the smoke touches the roof of the cave,
The green leaves burst into flames,
The air of night changes to dark water,
The mountains alter and become the sea.

JEROME ROTHENBERG

## THREE LANDSCAPES

### I

The dark bull quartered in my eye
turns slowly from his herd: the branches
part, and now his grey tongue,
trembling, fights a nest
of adders: stung,
the bloodroot quivers in the earth:
too late he walks along a
pebbled beach, his forehead
(like a grieving moon) against the sea.

### II

Tonight the river's warm with
bathers:
to throw myself against the rain,
be swallowed in its
darkness, like an eyelash.

### III.

White monks are climbing hills
inside her skull: the
fragile ash of love that falls in sleep,
as in the heart of laurel,
touched by drops of blood: so
too, within the cheek
of silence, beauty dressed in white
steps forth: in silence
forty monks await her on a ridge
of cinders, raising forty
candlesticks against the moon.

GEORGE KRESENKY

## THE SECOND WORLD WAR

Bull horns swallowing
The sea, in gardens of lettuce and green pools,
Among barbed wire, thrown down by the roses of the sea—
And now, bones of old men,
Smoking in the sun like pure fire
Floors of great ballrooms,
And women waltzing down an avenue of trees,
Surrounded by troops.

Germany, you have won the vineyards,
Whose grapes are pressed
In the sewers of Paris, and in your stone helmets,
While the tide races the horses near Mont St. Michel,
The birds rise from the blasted trees.

JAMES WRIGHT

## ON AN AMERICAN GIRL'S MARRIAGE

She dreamed long of waters.
Inland today, she wakens
On scraped knees, lost
Among locust thorns.

She feels for
The path backwards, to
The pillows of the sea.

Bruised trillium
Of wilderness, she may rest
On the briar leaves, as long as
The wind cares to pause.

Now she is going to learn
How it is that animals
Can save time:
They drowse a whole season
Of petty lamentation and snow
Without bothering to weep.

# SOME THOUGHTS ON LORCA AND RENÉ CHAR

THERE IS, IN AMERICA TODAY, a great enthusiasm for Garcia Lorca and René Char, and everyone would like to leap, at one bound, into their heaven. But why is it that France has produced a René Char, and we have not? The poetry of Lorca is poetry never seen before in any language. Char is really quite different from Apollinaire or Valery or Breton; how is it that they produce this, while the new poetry we produce is almost indistinguishable from that of twenty years ago, except that the formal patterns are stiffer?

It is evident to everyone that we have had no bold new poetry since the astounding daring of the *Wasteland*, published about 1922, which as Williams says, hit his contemporaries so hard they sat around simply staring at each other, or since the other daring poems published about that time, Williams' own poems, or Wallace Steven's delicate and reckless poems, or the *White Buildings*, published about 1926.

How is it, that in France, for instance, after having seen new poetry appear in the 1850's with Gautier and Baudelaire, in the 1860's with Verlaine and Mallarmé, in the 1880's with La Forgue and Rimbaud, then in 1913 with Apollinaire, in the 1920's with the surrealists, suddenly after the second World War, it appears again! And if we say the world situation is not propitious to the appearance of new poetry, well, it is obvious France lives in the same world we do! Let me ask the question again, how is it that Spain has produced Lorca, Hernandez, and many others; South America Neruda, Paz and many others; France, Char; while in America, after the rather dry flurry of leftist poetry in the thirties, which in imagination was quite sterile, poetry has been getting older and older every year, like a running down clock, until today even the younger poets are dissatisfied with their own work?

That is a serious question, and must have a serious answer, but the answer I would give is that these other poetries have passed through surrealism; we have not. Lorca was a friend of Salvador Dali; Char did not suddenly appear from the snow, and was not miraculously forged by the accident of war, as many suggest, but he wrote surrealist poetry for years before he wrote the poetry for which he is now famous. If you look at a bibliography, you will see that most of his early poems were published by 'Editions Surrealiste,' and that once, at least, he shared a book with Andre Breton and Paul Eluard. This to me has enormous significance. His early immersion in the surrealists is symbolic of the baptism of the entire French poetry of the nineteenth century in similar dark waters. Beginning with Baudelaire, French poetry went through a dark valley, a valley filled with black pools, lions, jungles, turbid rivers, dead men hanging from trees, wolves eating the feathers of birds, thunder hanging over doors, images of seas, sailors, drunken boats, maggots eating a corpse with the sound of a sower sowing grain, endless voyages, vast black skies, huge birds, continual rain. This immersion has given French poetry its strength, its rich soil, whereas our soil is thin and rocky, and the poetry of the 30's and 40's increasingly resembles a flower cut off above the ground, slowly withering.

We were not in a position before 1914 to understand what was going on in the new poetry, but afterwards we were. The astonishing revolution of imagination of 1914 came to us chiefly through Eliot and Pound, and it is unfortunate that both Eliot and Pound had a Puritan streak, which prevents their sinking deeper into the mind.

They both win the victory over the unconscious so easily. They somehow skip over the passions which Freud has described so well. Pound's poems, while they explore economic life, do not explore primitive depth of feeling; and Mr. Eliot finds it difficult to face Apeneck Sweeney, let alone the depths of Trakl or Neruda. In brief, the one tradition of modern poetry which they removed, as it passed through them, was the unconscious.

Even the Imagists were misnamed: they did not write in images from the unconscious, as Lorca or Neruda, but in simple pictures, such as 'petals on a wet black bough,' and Pound, for instance, continues to write in pictures, writing as great a poetry as is possible, which in his case is very great, using nothing but pictures, but still, pictures are not images. And without these true images, this water from the unconscious, the language continues to dry up.

In all men there is a struggle between the reason and the unconscious. In Eliot and Pound the mind won over the unconscious without too much struggle—the old Puritan victory. What they needed to balance their Puritanism is what France needed to balance her puritanism—namely, poems in which the unconscious wins out over the mind consistently, and that is precisely, of course, what 'surrealism' is.

We had in America thirty years ago on the one hand the ascetic poetry of the academic poets, and on the other hand the ascetic poetry of Pound and Eliot; and this has come down to us in the ascetic poetry of today, much of it noble. Still, it is surely possible to write other poetry than this also. Spanish poetry of this century, as in Lorca and Hernandez, seems to me even stronger than the French. The Spanish developed this poetry through Jimenez, Machado, Alberti, Lorca—a wholly different way; yet with only one thing in common: equally revolutionary, it was a sea poetry, a poetry of the unconscious, a poetry of water. It was what Lorca calls 'brown bread'; a poetry of seas and wolves,
of lost bells,
of lilies and bees
As Lorca says, 'Green, green, go deeper, green.'

*—Robert Bly*

Paul Celan

## CORONE

Aus der Hand frisst der Herbst mir sein Blatt: wir sind Freunde.
Wir schälen die Zeit aus den Nüssen und lehren sie gehn:
die Zeit kehrt zurück in die Schale.

Im Spiegel ist Sonntag,
im Traum wird geschlafen,
der Mund redet wahr.

Mein Aug steigt hinab zum Geschlecht der Geliebten:
wir sehen uns an,
wir sagen uns Dunkles,
wir lieben einander wie Mohn und Gedächtnis,
wir schlafen wie Wein in den Muscheln,
wie das Meer im Blutstrahl des Mondes.

Wir stehen umschlungen im Fenster, sie sehen uns zu von der Strasse:
es ist Zeit, dass man weiss!
Es ist Zeit, dass der Stein sich zu blühen bequemt,
dass der Unrast ein Herz schlägt.
Es ist Zeit, dass es Zeit wird.

Es ist Zeit.

Paul Celan

## CORONA

Autumn is eating a leaf from my hand; we are friends.
We are picking time out of a nut, we teach it to run:
and time rushes back to its shell.

In the mirror it's Sunday,
in dreams people sleep,
the mouth tells the truth.

My eye descends to the sex of my loved one,
we gaze at each other,
and speak in the darkness,
we love one another like poppies and memory,
we sleep like wine in a sea-shell
like the sea in the moon's bloody rays.

Embracing we stand in the window,
they look up at us from the street:
it is time that they knew!
It is time that the stone grew accustomed to blooming,
that unrest molded a heart.
It is time it was time.

It is time.

*From* Mohn und Gedachtnis,
*Deutsche Verlags-Anstalt,*
*Stuttgart, 1952. Translated*
*by Jerome Rothenberg.*

Paul Celan

## IN GESTALT EINES EBERS

In Gestalt eines Ebers
stampft dein Traum durch die Wälder am Rande des
                                                                     Abends.
Blitzendweiss
wie das Eis, aus dem er hervorbrach,
sind seine Hauer.

Eine bittere Nuss
wühlt er hervor unterm Laub,
dass sein Schatten den Bäumen entriss,
eine Nuss,
schwarz wie das Herz, das dein Fuss vor sich herstiess,
als du selber hier schrittst.

Er spiesst sie auf
und erfüllt das Gehölz mit grunzendem Schicksal,
dann treibts ihn
hinunter zur Küste,
dorthin, wo das Meer
seiner Feste finsterstes gibt
auf den Klippen:

vielleicht
dass eine Frucht wie die seine
das feiernde Auge entzückt,
das solche Steine geweint hat.

Paul Celan

## IN THE SHAPE OF A BOAR

In the shape of a boar
Your dream stamps through the woods on the
                      rim of the evening.
And his tusks,
Like the ice through which he has crashed,
Flash lightning.

He roots
For a bitter nut under the leaves
That his shadow tore down from a tree,
A nut
As black as the heart your foot kicked along
When you walked here yourself.

He gobbles it up
And fills those woods with his fateful grunting,
As it drives him
Below to the beach,
Far out where the sea
Is holding its gloomiest feast
On the reefs:

Perhaps
A fruit not unlike his own
Will enchant that celebrant's eye
Into weeping such stones as these.

*From* Von Schwelle zu Schwelle,
*Deutsche Verlags-Anstalt, Stuttgart,*
*1955. Translated by Jerome Rothenberg.*

PAUL CELAN

TODESFUGE

Schwarze Milch der Frühe wir trinken sie abends
wir trinken sie mittags und morgens wir trinken
                                        sie nachts
wir trinken und trinken
wir schaufeln ein Grab in den Lüften da liegt man
                                        nicht eng

Ein Mann wohnt im Haus der spielt mit den Schlangen
                                        der schreibt
der schreibt wenn es dunkelt nach Deutschland dein
                            goldenes Haar Margarete
er schreibt es und tritt vor das Haus und es blitzen
                die Sterne er pfeift seine Rüden herbei
er pfeift seine Juden hervor lässt schaufeln ein
                                Grab in der Erde
er befiehlt uns spielt auf nun zum Tanz

Schwarze Milch der Frühe wir trinken dich nachts
wir trinken dich morgens und mittags wir trinken
                                      dich abends
wir trinken und trinken

Paul Celan

## DEATH FUGUE

Black milk of morning we drink you at dusk
we drink you at noontime and dawntime we drink
                                            you at night
we drink and drink
we scoop out a grave in the sky where it's roomy
                                              to lie

There's a man in this house who cultivates
                               snakes and who writes
who writes when it's nightfall *nach Deutschland*
                            your golden hair Margareta
who writes it and walks from the house and the
stars all start flashing he whistles his dogs to
                                        draw near
whistles his Jews to appear starts us scooping a
                                    grave out of sand
he commands us to play for the dance

Black milk of morning we drink you at night
we drink you at dawntime and noontime we drink
                                      you at dusktime
we drink and drink

Ein Mann wohnt im Haus und spielt mit den Schlangen
der schreibt
der schreibt wenn es dunkelt nach Deutschland dein
goldenes Haar Margarete
Dein aschenes Haar Sulamith wir schaufeln ein Grab
in den Lüften da liegt man nicht eng

Er ruft stecht tiefer ins Erdreich ihr einen ihr
andern singet und spielt
er greift nach dem Eisen im Gurt er schwingts seine
Augen sind blau
stecht tiefer die Spaten ihr einen ihr andern spielt
weiter zum Tanz auf

Schwarze Milch der Frühe wir trinken dich nachts
wir trinken dich mittags und morgens wir trinken
dich abends
wir trinken und trinken
ein Mann wohnt im Haus dein goldenes Haar Margarete
dein aschenes Haar Sulamith er spielt mit den
Schlangen

Er ruft spielt süsser den Tod der Tod ist ein
Meister aus Deutschland
er ruft streicht dunkler die Geigen dann steigt ihr
als Rauch in die Luft
dann habt ihr ein Grab in den Wolken da liegt man
nicht eng

There's a man in this house who cultivates
                          snakes and who writes
who writes when it's nightfall *nach Deutschland*
                  your golden hair Margareta
your ashen hair Shulamite we scoop out a grave
            in the sky where it's roomy to lie

He calls jab it deep in the soil you men
                    you other men sing and play
he tugs at the sword in his belt he swings it
                          his eyes are blue
jab your spades deeper you men you other men
                  play up again for the dance

Black milk of morning we drink you at night
we drink you at noontime and dawntime we drink
                          you at dusktime
we drink and drink
there's a man in this house your golden hair
                                Margareta
your ashen hair Shulamite he cultivates snakes

He calls play that death thing more sweetly
Death is a gang-boss *aus Deutschland*
he calls scrape that fiddle more darkly then
                  hover like smoke in the air
then scoop out a grave in the clouds where it's
                              roomy to lie

Schwarze Milch der Frühe wir trinken dich nachts
wir trinken dich mittags der Tod ist ein Meister aus
                                                    Deutschland
wir trinken dich abends und morgens wir trinken und
                                                          trinken
der Tod ist ein Meister aus Deutschland sein Auge
                                                       ist blau
er trifft dich mit bleierner Kugel er trifft dich
                                               genau
ein Mann wohnt im Haus dein goldenes Haar Margarete
er hetzt seine Rüden auf uns er schenkt uns ein Grab
                                                   in der Luft
er spielt mit den Schlangen und träumet der Tod ist
                                      ein Meister aus Deutschland
dein goldenes Haar Margarete
dein aschenes Haar Sulamith

Black milk of morning we drink you at night
we drink you at noontime Death is a gang-boss
*aus Deutschland*
we drink you at dusktime and dawntime we
drink and drink
Death is a gang-boss *aus Deutschland* his eye
is blue
he hits you with leaden bullets his aim is
true
there's a man in this house your golden hair
Margareta
he sets his dogs on our trail he gives us a
grave in the sky
he cultivates snakes and he dreams Death is a
gang-boss *aus Deutschland*
your golden hair Margareta
your ashen hair Shulamite

*From* Mohn und Gedächtnis
*Deutsche Verlags-Anstalt,*
*Stuttgart, 1952. Translated*
*by Jerome Rothenberg.*

## THE NECESSITY OF REJECTING A SHAKESPEARE SONNET

THOM GUNN WROTE US RECENTLY, defending Yvor Winters, who turned up in the '*Wax Museum*', first issue, in the group of poems written without images, and Mr. Gunn included a sonnet of Shakespeare, which we quote below, asking us if we would include this also among the rejections.

> The expense of spirit in a waste of shame
> Is lust in action, and till action, lust
> Is perjured, murderous, bloody, full of blame,
> Savage, extreme, rude, cruel, not to trust,
> Enjoyed no sooner but despised straight,
> Past reason hunted, and no sooner had
> Past reason hated as a swallowed bait
> On purpose laid to make the taker mad.
> Mad in pursuit and in possession so,
> Had, having, and in quest to have, extreme,
> A bliss in proof, and proved a very woe;
> Before, a joy proposed; behind, a dream;
>   All this the world well knows, yet none knows well
>   To shun the heaven that leads men to this hell.

Such a sonnet as this was, at the time it was written, extremely interesting in language. At that time nothing was said directly in poetry; like a bird caught in the pattern of an Oriental rug, everything was wound in a thousand conceits, curleques, and intricate comparisons. If then Shakespeare writes something so bare as this, it is striking and new.

But now, 350 years later, everything, newspapers, reports, essays, scientific papers and poems are written in this same bare, direct, imageless style, and there is nothing new about it; it is exhausted, dead.

This is why we should be forced to send a rejection to Shakespeare should he send us one of his sonnets. But, of course, he wouldn't; he would write today in a language as fresh as his was in 1600. What that might be is hard to estimate, but I would guess it might resemble the language of Lorca or perhaps Neruda.

It seems to us dangerous to pretend that we live in Shakespeare's time, and that the problems of poetry and the language in which it is written are timeless. When one language dies, or is worn out, another must be used.

Now read Neruda on the same subject:

The evenings of the women-chasers and the nights of the
    conjugal couples
Join together like double bed-sheets to bury me;
And the hours . . when the bees have an odor of blood,
and the flies are buzzing in anger . . .
And still more, the adulterers who love each other with
    a true love
On beds high and huge as ocean liners;
This gigantic forest which is entangled and breathing
Hedges me around firmly on all sides forever
With huge flowers like mouths and false teeth
And black roots that take the shape of fingernails and shoes.

*From* Gentleman Alone *by Neruda.*

Passages written about death by both poets are also revealing:

Like as the waves make towards the pebbled shore,
So do our minutes hasten to their end;
Each changing place with that which goes before,
In sequent toil all forwards do contend.

      \*      \*      \*      \*

Lonely cemeteries exist,
Graves exist full of bones that do not make a sound,
The heart moving through a tunnel,
Darkness, darkness, darkness,
As in a shipwreck we die from the center,
As we drown in the chest,
As we go falling out of the skin into the soul.

Corpses exist,
Feet of cold and sticky clay exist,
Death exists inside the bones,
Like a pure sound,
Like a barking where there are no dogs,
Coming out from more than one bell, from more than one
    grave,
Swelling in the damp air like tears or rain.
I see, alone, sometimes
Coffins with sails. . . .

*From* Death Alone *by Neruda.*

Mirko Tuma

## DOPIS

Po prvé
jsem Tě zahlédl
v bolesti zrna přezrálého.
Slunce paličkovalo zlatými jehlami
krajku polí a lesů
a zahrad navlhlých
rosou.

Po prvé
jsem Te oslovil
v klenutí gotického paláce
nahlodaného poesií
čtyřiadvacetihodinové noci,
kde ženy jež nikdy neotevřely květ ruze
tančily po zvrácených snech
a chlapi s ohořelou
skořápkou srdce
řešili na žlutých prostěradlech
hlavolam stesku.

Mirko Tuma

## LETTER

I first
glimpsed you
when I lived in the pain of the seed which is too ripe.
The sun with gold needles wove
a lace of fields and woods
and orchards that the dew
has moistened.

I first
spoke to you
in the arched hall of a gothic castle
which the poetry of night
was eating away,
where women who have never opened the foliage of a rose
danced on the tiles of twisted dreams
and men with heartshells burnt to ashes
solved on yellow bedsheets
the enigma of loneliness.

Pastorální symfonie
jak pramen vytrysklý z panenských rukou
rozložila ocel nemocničních postelí
blesky se zavěsily na větvích
jediného stromu.
Cosi jak naděje slzelo
v zamřižovaném zrcadle. . . .

Po prvé
jsem Ti psal
když ses dotýkala hladového prachu
větrné růžice . . .
Doma, daleko doma
zavoněla louka procitlá
a v hromu jenž přezvučel
moře
poslala pozdrav sněženek a bezu.

The Pastoral Symphony
like a river blossoming from the palms of a virgin
dissolved the steel of the beds of hospitals
and lightning clashes clustered on the branches
of that lone tree.
Something like hope wept
in the looking glass with bars . . .

I first
wrote to you
when you were touching the starving dust
of weathervanes . . .
At home, far away home
a stirring meadow started to give off its scent
and by thunder stronger than the sound of the sea
sent a message
of snowflakes and lilacs.

Klenutí gotcikého paláce
otevřelo hamižnou náruč
nedostupnému slunci
a v rozhovorech pološeptaných
a poloúzkostných
přec zněly varhany.
Velikonoční branou
pršely obrazy
mátožných početí.
Stárnutí, lasko . . . .

Boyhně odmítáni
kula
v Hefaistově dílně
železo žhavé lži,
Nesmírná Čekání
na vodu chladící,
potůček čirý
s žilnatými oblásky
narozenými
pod víčky sudiček . . .

The arch of the gothic palace
opened his miserly arms apart
to the unapproachable sun
and even in the talks half-whispered
and half-afraid
the organ was sounding.
Through the Easter gate
images rained down
of exhausted conceivings.
Aging, my love . . .

The Goddess of No
smelted together
in the fires of Hephestus
iron of a lie that burns.
The huge Waiting
for a water that cools
for a clear brook
with stones of delicate veins
born
in the bags under the eyes of women who foretell at birth . . .

Mirko Tuma

## POÈME

Bližší než noc . . . a zákmit . . . jiskření,
Krev žhavá mlčením,
Má poesie,
Včela zabloudilá k svatozáři žárovky,
k nahému prsu světélkujícímu
uprostřed moře.

Mirko Tuma

## POEM

Closer than the night . . . and flesh . . . throwing off sparks
Blood boiling from holding the voices in,
My poetry,
A bee who lost his way and wound up on the halo of a
    light bulb,
On a naked breast sparkling
In the middle of the sea.

> *From* Jedenáctá Ulice, *Kruh
> Prátel Ceské Poesie, New York,
> 1954, translated by Robert Bly.*

# THE WORK OF DONALD HALL

I AM NEVER ABLE TO READ THE POEMS of Donald Hall without having many thoughts about the middle class, and it is possible that it is just such thoughts that the poems are intended to evoke. Some critics, especially in the universities, maintain that poetry should restrain itself to words, sounds, myths, etc., and evoke only universal and timeless thoughts, but such a theory is too grotesque. Mr. Hall, at least, has gotten himself involved in a very interesting subject matter. It is as if in his work poetry and the middle class had taken a vow not to destroy each other.

It is as if many years ago in some dark forest as in the Grimm brothers, the American poets founded a compact 'dedicated to the proposition that the wage-earners and poetry shall not kill each other on contact, but shall strengthen and nourish each other.' And we are somehow gathered, for the last ten years, to see if this proposition is true or not. It is amazing how much pressure is brought to bear on this proposition. When Wallace Stevens died, *Time* magazine concluded, somewhat prematurely perhaps, that his life showed 'there was no conflict between business and poetry.'

All through American life, of the nineteenth century or the twentieth, interest always appears in the relationship of the poet to the middle class, or the business class, or the believers in security, or however else one might describe them and one reason it comes up so often obviously is that in America the poet has never had an existence in people's minds independent from the middle class or any other class. There has never been the concept of the poet here that there is, for instance, in Ireland. Yeats always said that the great thing about Ireland was that the ancient concept of the poet or bard, as a being apart from all classes, himself, with a kind of grandeur, still somehow lived in Ireland. Yeats himself simply, as he said, stepped into that role, and from that role learned how to imagine himself. The poet in Ireland was imagined by the people to be a kind of creature which could best, strangely enough, be described by the word 'poet', and he was expected to be bold, passionate with women, outspoken against the powerful, having a knowledge of the inner life, dangerous, capable of magic, and with a mysterious love of music and water.

America can obviously give her poets no such help, since she has never imagined any firm image of what a poet might be. It is in this century for the first time in America that any image of the poet is developing at all. France has always had her vision of the poet, a position becoming now increasingly high and inaccessible, like some mountain flower; and anyone who knows Spanish literature knows Spain's image of the poet, as the most intelligent, the most solitary, the most active, and the most *alive* person in the country. In South America, as I understand it, the poet, because his feelings are living, is always thought of as the defender of the poor, and the enemy of the rich. Both Vallejo and Neruda obviously think of themselves in this way.

America certainly has no firm image of this kind. A nincompoop like Longfellow hardly lends himself to any definition, and in this period every generation, Whittier, Whitman, Robinson, seemed to present, and did present, a totally different picture of the poet.

Since the dominant class in America was always the middle or business class, the meaning of such variety was that the American poet has never declared his independence from this class. Whitman did, saying that the poet's place was nearer to working men and animals.

> I think I could turn and live with animals, they are so placid and self-contained,
> I stand and look at them long and long.
> They do not sweat and whine about their condition,
> They do not lie awake in the dark and weep for their sins,
> They do not make me sick discussing their duty to God,
> Not one is dissatisfied, not one is demented with the mania of owning things,
> Not one kneels to another, nor to his kind that lived thousands of years ago,
> Not one is respectable or unhappy over the whole earth.

Also:

> I am enamor'd of growing out-doors,
> Of men that live among cattle, or taste of the oceanwoods
> Of the builders and steerers of ships and the wielders
>     of axes and mauls, and the drivers of horses;
> I can eat and sleep with them week in and week out.

But the critics, rather than emphasizing that distinction, so that the sense of a poet can take root, are themselves middle class; they have erased as rapidly as possible any distinction between Whitman and the middle class; and they have made Whitman to appear comfort-loving, a sentimentalist, 'the good gray poet,' etc. Consequently, one peculiarity of America at the beginning of the century was that no secure place for the poet had been imagined.

IN THE 1910's, THE POETS SUCH AS Eliot and Pound, instead of facing that prospect, go abroad, and gradually the concept of the poet becomes associated with the 'exile', which is certainly a ridiculously insecure way for a country to imagine its poets. Nevertheless, this concept of the poet as 'exile' is the first firm image we have, and Eliot's taking out English citizenship and Pound's going to Italy merely strengthen it, and even Hemingway's first success in Paris strengthens it. One reason these poets dominate over the stay-at-home poets like Frost and Stevens is that they provide a colourful picture of the poet, and one easily remembered: he is the one too sensitive for American life, the speaker of many languages, the romantic rover, as in a Henry James novel, the fierce traitor eating his heart out, or the one man standing alone against his country.

This concept began to break up in the thirties as the poets began coming back, though some stay-at-homes such as Cummings still keep to that concept in an invisible way, and Cummings' books more and more resemble a message from some other planet, even written differently than books written here on earth.

Crane is an exception. His concept of the poet, adventurer in experience, based on Whitman, has great vigor, but he of course dies very young, and poetry is then left in the hands of various poets and critics who, after the leftist infatuation, which dies down, present no clear image of the poet at all. But poets such as Eberhart, Shapiro, and to some extent, Rexroth, by the examples of their lives gradually establish the idea of the poet as a happily married man. Through emphasis on family and children, they somehow keep the folk and individual roots of which the thirties thought highly, and the position seems to present the possibility of getting nearer the basic life of the country than the position of the poet as exile.

The poet as job-holding, family man is the way by which, for lack of alternatives, the poet had already been imagined by Ransom and Van Doren, etc., so the two branches join and take firm root. In my opinion, this idea of the poet is still the one which prevails and has prevailed well into the fifties. The poet as a happy member of the middle class, participating in PTA, car-buying, and the general worship of children, is of course a very different thing from Yeats the poet being married, whose marriage is often brought up to defend all sorts of common-place living. Yeats carried his concept of the poet into marriage with him, instead of improvising as he went along. This concept of the poet as a useful citizen and family man is still with us, and Lowell's poems about adultery, and Snodgrass's poems about divorce are really written unconsciously against the usually accepted background of the happily married poet.

A great deal was lost in the shift from one concept of the poet to the other, including the influence of European poetry on American, which in 1920 was rapidly increasing, and which now, in my opinion, has virtually died out; and also the poet's 'aloneness', his existence as a sort of lonely mountain full of opinions which no one else shares, which is as true of Jeffers as of Eliot and Pound. The most important thing that was lost seems to me to be that independence from the 'middle class' which the concept 'exile' somehow carried with it.

One of the valuable gifts carried along with the modern movement in Europe was the poet's independence from the majority, or from the middle class, as in the case of Baudelaire, who established it through sheer savagery—

insulting the middle class right and left with what it least likes to hear, with poems about corpses, or love affairs with mulatto women, or poems about Lesbianism, or huge insults to democracy. Even his form at that time was somehow an insult. Valery, who did what the business class never does—spent all his time thinking—was equally savage in his way. When the modern movement did come to America, in the persons of Eliot and Pound, about 1914, a certain independence was carried with it. Unfortunately, Pound and Eliot did not themselves stay in America, and the most evident thing of the last thirty years would seem to be that the modern movement never became fully established in America, and moreover, seems to have died about ten years ago, after a near-zombie life for another previous ten years. There is the sense that the poets of the fifties must go through this agonizing separation again, and live through these transformations of modern poetry once more.

My point is that the absence of Eliot and Pound, the early death of Crane, and to a degree, Eliot's active effort in his criticism to stop the modern movement in the English language, had all, by 1950, contributed to a strange position. Poetry, at the beginning of the fifties, had slipped back to the old situation before Baudelaire, when poetry and the middle class were living in an uneasy bliss. Poetry was writing itself in nice iambic lines, which the middle class in America had always loved, and with which it was long familiar; in rhymes, the absence of which in poems makes the middle class very nervous; and in content, it tried to be modern without offending anyone. I think Ciardi's work is a good example of this sort of poetry of the early fifties. He wrote cheerfully about the war, his children and his students, and he glorified marriage. We notice that he is now poetry editor of the *Saturday Review*, and that his current book is called *I Marry You*, in which the word 'you' seems to refer both to his wife and to the middle class.

The effort of the poets of the fifties has been to pull themselves out of this soggy ground. The work and development of almost any vigorous poet of the fifties, W. D. Snodgrass or Gary Snyder or Robert Creeley or

Louis Simpson or James Wright, particularly his recent work, are equally revealing from this point of view.

We are considering here Mr. Hall, and it is very curious that both the two 'concepts' of the American poet discussed here appear in the title of Mr. Hall's first book *Exiles and Marriages*, as if he were wavering between the two, or did not feel very secure in either. *Exiles and Marriages* is a large book, and has some sections such as the light-verse section, #4, which should have been omitted entirely. The sections most interesting to me are 5 and 6, which could just as well have been called 'Problems of the Middle Class'. As we are reading in these sections, we begin to notice something standing above us, looking over our shoulders. The poet himself notices this, and writes:

> Over my bed
> Last night there stood
> The form I dread
> Of Father God.

This sense, throughout the book, becomes oppressive. As it grows stronger we realize that something other than God is looking down also. God, Freud says, is usually imagined as a father, and since the father is always the one who upholds the rules and duties of the society, the father may become an unconscious symbol of society itself. We soon become aware at least that the figure looking down at us with accusing eyes is not only father God, but it is the actual father himself. The poet notices this also, and says:

> Over my bed
> My father stood
> Fixed in the stead
> Of abstract God.

Throughout these poems we feel again and again the 'classic' hatred of the father, and restlessness under his authority. The first poem in the section is called 'The Sleeping Giant', which is the name of a bluff near the childhood home of the poet. In this poem the fear of the father is transmuted into the fear of the 'Giant'.

> I was afraid the waking arm would break
> From the loose earth and rub against his eyes
> A fist of trees, and the whole country tremble
> In the exultant labor of his rise;
>
> Then he with giant steps in the small streets
> Would stagger, cutting off the sky, to seize
> The roofs from house and home because we had
> Covered his shape with dirt and planted trees; . . .
>
> That was the summer I expected him.
> Later the high and watchful sun instead
> Walked low behind the house, and school began,
> And winter pulled a sheet over his head.

The last stanza contains a faintly disguised wish for the death of the father, which is again a perfectly natural one. We therefore notice the same thing as in the poems on God, namely a rejection. As he writes in another poem which is really a rejection of God:

> If there is no justice
> Where great Jehovah is
> I will the devil kiss.

If Freud is right, we should expect the same feelings toward society itself, a sense of hostility and of being boxed in. In a poem called 'The Strangers', Mr. Hall writes:

> O garden of strangers, declensions
>     Of face repeating face
> I walked through the rushing of flowers
>     To meet your race. . . .
>
> I wanted to enter your garden
>     And join your single state
> But rank upon rank of your sameness
>     Secured the gate.

In another poem, speaking of writing poetry, we have the same sense of a closed door:

> Mine the loud wind in pain—
> The worded room will yield
> Your canny agony
> Not excellence nor will.

In the long poem in section 6, called 'Exile', he describes the terrible isolation that many people in the middle or business classes feel. By 'exile' he describes a strange state of mind in which nothing seems real, neither death nor life. The present is scorned for something ahead in the future, one girl is scorned for another. Gradually the real world is abandoned, and another world is imagined, in which the speaker is a hero, and in this 'manufactured country' 'none of us can break the walls to talk'.

The poem closes with a description of this terrible isolation, often thought of as characteristic of the 'easy-living' class today:

> We are as solitary as the dead,
> Wanting to king it in that perfect land
> We make and understand.
> And in this world whose pattern is unmade,
> Phases of splintered light and shapeless sand,
> We shatter through our motions and evade
> Whatever hand might reach and touch our hand.

At any rate, this triumvirate of Father, God, and middle class society are the three great giants in this book, and toward all three the poet has the same mingled longing and loathing. In a later poem in this section he concludes:

> The blind upon the blind
> Only conceive the blind.

The way out of this impasse is conceived to be the will. We become very conscious of will. He says:

> I pray the will may be
> More powerful.

and:

> The will is enemy
> To the mere vanity.

We understand that the strict use of meters is a part of this will, but the will somehow does not seem to give promise of succeeding. The last sentence in the book is: 'May I earn an honest eye'. We are again surprised that he does not ask for what we would expect a poet to ask for, a great imagination, secret powers, passionate love. What he asks for, a conscious honesty, is again associated with the will.

The book had a strange reviewing history. *Time* magazine suddenly gave it a review of some length, unusual for a first book, and praised it. *Time* being what it is, and despised by most intelligent people in the country, its praise virtually destroyed at one stroke Mr. Hall's reputation as a poet. This strange attraction was followed by equally strange repulsions. A professor at the University of Chicago named Richard Stern, recently involved also in the 'suppression' of the *Chicago Review*, on the faculty side, wrote an article called 'The Poetry of Donald Hall' for the *Chicago Review*, Summer, 1956. Here he quoted lines, and followed them mainly with catty remarks such as 'Our dear President could not have said it better'. It is clear that neither he nor *Time* was responding to the poetry, but rather to something involving the middle class.

The book was also praised and blamed for its use of traditional meters. But we can see the heavy use of 'traditional' meters in the fifties in a new light. The 'traditions' in question are not deeply American, but come from English poetry, and of course, for us the *cultural* 'father' is English. Iambic meter is used not only because it is the only well-developed meter in the language, but also it is used pyschologically, so to speak, to avoid offending the English. Since within us, the English, the dominating middle class society, God, and the father, all mean the same, the iamb serves the purpose of avoiding offense to all these three. Actually, if the marriage with the middle class was to continue, some method of avoiding offense had to be found. Several methods were found, and one of them was traditional meters.

I HAVE TRIED TO ESTABLISH THAT THERE was in the early fifties a sort of marriage of the poet and the middle class society, of which Mr. Hall's first book, published in 1955, was a good example, as were other books of James Wright, Philip Booth, etc. This poetic marriage with the middle class has finally begun to break up, as in 1910, perhaps this time for good. It is a general movement, not confined to any one poet, and we should not be surprised to see some rather sharp criticisms of the same middle class appear in Mr. Hall's second book, published in 1958. Its title, again rather symbolically, is *The Dark Houses*, perhaps the houses darkened to see TV better, or the houses that as another poet said, 'darken in their sleep of death'. *The Dark Houses* has two sections, and again it is the first section, the poems whose subject is the middle class, which interests me most. There the criticism is considerably sharper than in the first book. In a poem called 'The Adults' there is a poignant picture of the poet as a child lying alone at night hearing the 'social' voices of the grown-ups:

> I remember hearing their voices talk
> downstairs, while I listened awake in my bed,
> not understanding particular words, but the pitch
> of the laughter, the lies, the responsive pitches.

This could have been spoken by one of the characters in *Main Street*, and it is evident that poetry is taking over now some of the functions of 'social criticism' which the novel used to handle. Another poem called 'The Family' is really, strangely enough, a rather good short story in verse. It begins:

> Under the glassy Christmas tree
> the packages wait for Daddy
>     who is asleep. He remembers,
> gripping the sheet, some old story
>
> in which he eats his own mother's
> affable dog, yet is it hers
>     or his, or his kids' dog, or his
> kids themselves that he eats?

It closes:

> Each kid will look at each parent
>
> for a while, and go out (listen
> to their motorcycles!) and then
>     return to sit in a huddle,
> also drunk. He looks to straighten
>
> His tie, now, and descends to fill
> his stomach with oat cereal.
>     He is hungry, very hungry;
> He thinks he could eat an animal.

In '1934' Mr. Hall describes what his grandparents' farm in Vermont was like during the Depression. When hobos came to the door, these old New Englanders were not moved by compassion or love:

> My father said they might
> Burn us and all the cattle up at night,
> If we refused them food.

From the point of view of these old Vermonters, the Model A's were 'Fouled by the eagles of the NRA'. Mr. Hall ends the poem with a strange insult, saying they were the kind of people who, during the Depression, got mail.

The sense of isolation from any real world, which was described in the first book as Exile, he now sees is not peculiar to the suburbs or to the 1950's. The first poem in the book is a sort of history of the last forty years of a little Connecticut town called Whitneyville (where the first mass-produced firearms were made, made by of all people Eli Whitney). This history is remembered at the grave of the poet's father, a businessman who had died shortly before. The poem, in some sense an elegy, is a very interesting piece of writing. As a poem, it suffers, I think, from being jammed into the strict iambic pentameter four line rhymed stanza, which gives it the effect of having all been read before, and seriously cuts down on its freshness. Nevertheless, despite this, the poet can still occasionally write fine and heartbreaking lines:

'The things you had to miss,' you said last week,
'Or thought you had to, take your breath away.'

He concludes the poem by saying:

The stones are white, the grass is black and deep . . .
The lights go out and it is Christmas day.

The last poem in the book is a vision, for the first time in Hall's work, of a kind of life richer than all this.

> He
> expects that when he finds it,
> it will be
> like a man, visible, alive
> to what has happened and what
> will happen, with
> firmness in its face. . . . .

It is also unquestionably the best poem in the book. There is some suggestion of an inward life. There is no mention of 'will' anymore, as a way out, or as a way to conquer weakness. It is interesting too that this poem is the one most free of the pesty iambs, which as we suggested before, are themselves a kind of 'will'.

One senses through both books that the poetry is often strengthened by its subject of the middle class, but that poetry about the middle class, whether praising or attacking, is not an end in itself; for the poetry that gets too near the middle class here is often swallowed by it. There is no doubt that there is a progression in Mr. Hall's work. In his first book, he often spoke of the poet and the majority of people as 'we'; this is not found in the second book, where the two begin to distinguish themselves. His poems, especially in the first section of the last book, are still a mixture of poetry and the middle class, and after reading even some of the poems in *The Dark Houses*, we realize that the feeling we get from some of them is not the feeling we get from poetry. In other words, he is still so troubled by some of these problems, that instead of writing a poem, he simply writes something about the middle class, using the same form as one would use if one were writing a poem. It is interesting then, that in the poems written after the book, there is no mention of the middle class at all. There is a recent poem called 'The Long River' which I will quote entire:

### The Long River

The musk-ox smells
in his long head
my boat coming. When
I feel him there,
intent, heavy,

the oars make wings
in the white night,
and brave woods are close
on either side
where trees darken.

I rowed past towns
in their black sleep
to come here. I passed
the northern grass
and cold mountains.

The musk-ox moves
when the boat stops,
in hard thickets. Now
the wood is dark
with old pleasures.

One surprising quality in Mr. Hall is that like most of the poets of his generation, and in contrast to those of the thirties and forties, he seems capable of development and of movement.

THIS MUST BE THE END OF THE LITTLE tour, which could be called 'adventures of the American poet trying to imagine himself'. I think the opposite of the theory with which we began has been proved; namely, it seems from the experience of the last ten years that poetry and the middle class are incompatible. Some clearer image of the poet is needed.

Actually a new concept of the poet is beginning to develop, that of the homosexual hipster, but this concept is really as far from the concept of the poet that America needs and her poets need, as that of the happily-married-man poet. It is again an evasion of the problem of the poet living in a country like America.

It is possible that we are also seeing the development of a new feeling of a poet as one independent from the middle class, in fact a critic of the middle class. Much work of recent years would seem to share in this, including such strangely assorted poets as Thomas McGrath, Leslie Woolf Hedley, Lawrence Ferlinghetti, W. S. Merwin in his most recent poems, Louis Simpson in some of his work, and Kenneth Rexroth. Mr. Hall appears to be moving toward this independent state also, though we feel so far that he has been criticizing the middle class from *inside* the middle class. Since the country has no image of a poet as a poet, a poet to develop must learn to imagine himself, and to do this, it may be necessary for the poet to decide more clearly what the middle class *is*, and what the poet is. Making this distinction is complicated by the fact that many poets, Mr. Hall among them, have made their living so far working in what we have called 'the middle class' as professors. But the poet is one who devotes his whole life to poetry; it is not merely to bring poetry into one's life, but to change the whole thing into poetry, and it is possible that to do that one must leave the middle class entirely, and all its ideas and securities.

At any rate, it is clear that the younger poets are dividing into two groups now, those in favor of a different kind of poetry than has been written, and those firmly opposed to any 'experimentation'. Such poets as John Hollander and Thom Gunn are clearly in the second group. In a review of *Dark Houses* in *Partisan Review*, John Hollander, for instance, writes: 'One can only hope' that these (more experimental poems) of Mr. Hall 'represent a short blind alley jutting out from the course of a long and distinguished body of work'. How can a poet who has one moderately good book to date, have 'a long and distinguished body of work' behind him? It is absurd. Such statements are made in an effort to discourage poets from further experimentation. Nevertheless, recent poems of Mr. Hall, such as 'Snow' and the poem quoted here, 'The Long River', are clearly a movement into something new.

>     The musk-ox moves
>     When the boat stops,
>     In hard thickets. Now
>     The woods are dark
>     With old pleasures.

This poem seems to me by many times the finest poem he has written, and at the same time the poem of his which is most completely a poem. It also suggests that the way out of the middle class is by a door the middle class cannot find—a secret life. The concept of the poet as a man with an inner life is, as we look back, the central quality of a poet as developed by Yeats, and the Spanish, and this image seems the one least developed in America.

—CRUNK

# FOUR CITY POEMS

Louis Simpson

## CHAMBER OF DEPUTIES

Do you remember the
Sleeping city
Street of the Skeleton
Red gutters of
The grand butchery
Odors of love?

Under the cross
Of the flayed horse
Gutted and splayed
And the hooked pig
There there it was
Your breasts grew big.

Blood laps our bones
As Seine her stones
In a cold sleep
We laugh and sing
Lake ragged crones
Who dream of spring.

The morning sun
Is made of iron
At eight o'clock
And the brass helmets
Ride on ride on
To the Chamber of Deputies.

Davɪd Ignatow

## THE DREAM

Someone approaches to say his life is ruined
and to fall down at your feet
and pound his head upon the sidewalk.
Blood spreads in a puddle.
And you, in a weak voice, plead
with those nearby for help;
your life takes on his desperation.
He keeps pounding his head.
It is you who are fated;
and you fall down beside him.
It is then you are awakened,
the body gone, the blood washed from the ground,
the stores lit up with their goods.

## THE ESCAPADE

Poet and gangster reach in the dark;
blind flashes reveal them.
The dead collapse
and the living scatter for cover.
Alone now, they think the street is theirs
and swiftly make their getaway,
in the left hand the haul,
in the right jammed in the driver's back
the weapon as they careen;
and at the hideout set up
to repel the law—coming nearly as swift
sirening. In the inferno,
started by both sides, riddled,
still seeking to shoot,
they sink to their deaths,
the haul beside them still theirs.

Denise Levertov

## FEBRUARY EVENING IN NEW YORK

As the stores close, a winter light
  opens air to iris blue,
  glint of frost through the smoke,
  grains of mica, salt of the sidewalk.
As the buildings close, released autonomous
  feet pattern the streets
  in hurry and stroll; balloon heads
  drift and dive above them; the bodies
  aren't really there.
As the lights brighten, as the sky darkens,
  a woman with crooked heels says to another woman
  while they step along at a fair pace,
  'You know, I'm telling you, what I love best
  is life. I love life! Even if I ever get
  to be old and wheezy—or limp! You know?
  Limping along?—I'd still. . . .' Out of hearing.
To the multiple disordered tones
  of gear changing, a dance,
  to the compass points, out, four-way river.
  Prospect of sky
  wedged into avenues, left at the ends of streets,
  west sky, east sky: more life tonight! A range
  of open time at winter's outskirts.

# A NOTE ON HYDROGEN BOMB TESTING

WE HAVE RECEIVED LETTERS ASKING WHY, if we are *poets*, we concern ourselves with the activities of the Atomic Energy Commission. We believe that artists above all are not exempt from fighting in national issues. The greatest poets, Yeats among them, have opposed their government, or any organ of it, which was harmful to the people. Americans as a whole have been too much trained toward *tolerance*; when a false shepherd calls, they follow along like sheep. Condonement of the policies of the A.E.C. would be a poor show of love for the United States.

The A.E.C. has lied directly, as in the case when, under Lewis Strauss, it gave evidence that we could not complete an explosion-ban with the Russians, because a recent test in Nevada proved that an underground explosion could be heard only two hundred and fifty miles away. Senator Humphrey found out the explosion had been heard in Alaska, 2,500 miles away, whereupon the A.E.C. explained that a clerical error of one zero had been made. The Commission has unscrupulously poo-pooed any anxiety over the effects of radiation on human and animal health.

We believe that poisoning and mutating children who aren't even born yet, in this country and elsewhere, is an immoral act, regardless of the circumstances. Yet no major stand on the part of any mass medium or by any church in the United States has been made against the A.E.C. On the contrary, Linus Pauling's statements were given minimal—even deprecatory—coverage, whereas *Life* honored and supported Dr. Teller, including his statement that fallout from a hydrogen bomb is no more dangerous than a radium wrist watch.

In both Russia and America the scientific mind, with its passion for experiment and its confusion on moral issues, is being allowed to become a decisive factor, even the mentor of state policy. In the Middle Ages the Church ruled society, carrying out any experiments it wished; today the scientists experiment as they wish. Just as the Church was indifferent to freedom of thought, scientists like those of the Atomic Energy Commission are indifferent to human suffering. Unless these men are fought, in their inquisition millions will die.

# Madame Tussaud's Wax Museum

SOME PEOPLE GO SO FAR AS TO SAY that academic poetry does not exist; we wouldn't go quite that far; in fact, it seems obvious that academic poetry not only exists here but has numerous grandparents. Perhaps it is the grandchild of the old 'poetic' poetry, in which all sorts of rhymes, middle names for the poets, inverted sentences, archaic usages, Sunday-afternoon meters and bashful language were used to make the poetry more poetic. Unfortunately these grandchildren of the old poetic poetry are now the judges and sponsors for the new poetry in America. The Lamont Poetry Prize is becoming more absurd every time it is given, and with respect to John Hall Wheelock, the poetry he publishes is for the most part archaic and decrepit.

> We break the glass, whose sacred wine
>     To some beloved health we drain,
> Lest future pledges, less divine,
>     Should e'er the hallowed toy profane.
>             *Edward Coote Pinkney*, 1802-28.

> Equilibrists, lie here; stranger, tread light;
> Close, but untouching in each other's sight;
> Mouldered the lips and ashy the tall skull,
> Let them lie perilous and beautiful.
>
>             *John Crowe Ransom, editor of the* Kenyon Review, *Lines taken from* Understanding Poetry, *Brooks and Warren.*

O restless, homeless human soul,
Following for aye thy nameless quest,
The gulls float, and the billows roll;
Thou watchest still, and questionest:-
Where is thy mate, and where thy nest?
                *Elizabeth Akers Allen, 1832-1911.*

Time the inflammable, the fragrant burden
Of star and flower, in the sky and garden.
The summer is a night, so swiftly slow
Does the one tempo of the movement flow.

        *Louise Townsend Nicholl, one of the judges of the Lamond Poetry Prize. Lines from* New Poems by American Poets, # 2, *edited by Rolfe Humphries, 1957.*

Methinks ofttimes my heart is like some bee
That goes forth through the summer days and sings. . . .
            *Ella Wheeler Wilcox, 1850-1919.*

For, as all flesh must die, so all,
Now dust, shall live. 'Tis natural;
Yet hardly do I understand—. . . .

        *John Hall Wheelock, editor of the* Poets of Today *series for Scribners, Lines from* The Winged Horse Anthology, *edited by Auslander and Hill, Doubleday, 1950.*

# THE OTHER NIGHT IN HEAVEN

## By Diana Tilling

(For our readers who might have missed the incredible article in the Spring *Partisan Review*, we present a version below.)

My name is Diana Tilling and I am very important. My husband is Lionel Tilling, and he is also very important. Between the two of us, we are so important that everything we do, think, or say deserves a lot of space in the *Partisan Review*.

The other night the 'Beats' were to read their poetry at Columbia, and we three wives of the English Department decided to go. Ginsberg was an old student of my husband's years ago. Ginsberg wanted terribly to be like the teachers at Columbia; I saw that even then. He always wanted to serve perfect martinis, and eat dinner on East Indian plates, and have famous friends like us. It is a shame that Ginsberg didn't turn out to be more like Lionel, when he had such a perfect model!

How different it might have been for Ginsberg and his friends if they had been born ten or fifteen years sooner! That was one of the particular sadnesses of the other evening. That they weren't born before the thirties was a real loss; they should at least have tried to. If they had, they could have sung union songs, played mah-jong, and been great rebels like us! They could have criticized Freud, and ended up running the *Partisan Review*, like Lionel and me. They could even have looked down on Frost! All their poems would have been much better if they had been written in our generation. In those days, in the wonderful thirties, one never had to be lonely. The intellectuals were never depressed in the Depression. But these Beats were good boys, even if they were lonely.

If these boys were good, why did Jimmy Hoffa, whom I met on the street that afternoon, tell me he was ashamed that I was attending that night? Why did Prince Rainier chide me, and why did Herman Hesse and Charlie Chaplin and W. H. Auden try to dissuade me? All these people, my friends, were wearing new clothes. All intellectuals do this. It is one of the rewards of being a successful writer in America.

Perhaps I wander. It was all a matter of finance that brought Ginsberg to Columbia that Thursday night. Just before we left, the maid had cleaned our house. Our house is always comfortable and clean. (That is the reward of being a successful writer in America). For me, it was of some note that the auditorium smelled fresh when I arrived. I took one look at the crowd and was certain that it would smell bad. Columbia students are all so dirty. Nevertheless, they smelled all right. The audience was clean and Ginsberg was clean and Corso was clean and Orlovsky was clean, and the kitchen was clean and the politics were clean and we were all good clean Americans. All intellectuals are clean.

My next great worry was, how did *I* look to the Beats? I mean, can they see that I am important, that I am a wife to the English Department, in fact that I *am* the English Department? Did I look like a Faculty Wife? The students didn't even recognize me! Lionel will flunk them all. I looked around, and luckily saw dear Norman. (Norman Podhoretz, born 1930, critic for the *Partisan Review*, and an old student of Lionel's. He is not in our generation, but a darling boy anyway.)

The poets were to be introduced by Fred Dupee, a very close friend of my husband's, and his wife Andy was with me. And how about Dupee, whom I have made an ass of by dragging him into this article—how would Dupee fare? What was he doing back there with all those terrible people?

Pity is very hard for most people, especially those born after the thirties. When the poets came out, I discovered something. All these poets are children! They wanted their bottles! I know that what I wanted to do was to go up on the stage, bundle Allen up, take him home, and feed him warm milk.

The biggest thrill of the evening came when Ginsberg

read a poem for my Lionel. It was entitled 'Go Home, Lionel', and it nearly moved me to tears. The poem had all the passion, goodness, sympathy, thankfulness, the wonderfulness, the hopefuless, the Thirties-quality, of any decent poem. The others then read, and then the question period came. Now at last Ginsberg was able to be a real teacher, like the professors at Columbia.

The evening over, we returned to our homes. When I got home, I found in our comfortably-furnished living room a comfortable professional meeting going on. I found there Pope John, Charlie Chaplin, Boris Pasternak, Daddy Warbucks, William Phillips, Randall Jarrell, Smiling Jack, W. H. Auden, Henry Ford, Picasso, The Dean of Canterbury, Mao Tse Tung, The Wright Brothers, The Hathaway Man, Jacques Barzun, Stephen Markmus, Robert Hall, and Henry Luce. To find your living-room so full is the reward of being a successful writer in America. (Stephen Markmus, born 1932. Old student of Lionel's. He reviews for the *Partisan Review*.) I said to Lionel, 'Allen Ginsberg read a love-poem to you, Lionel. I liked it very much.' It was a strange thing to say in the circumstances, perhaps even a little foolish. But I'm sure that Ginsberg's old teacher knew what I, as a wife of the English Department, was saying, and why I was impelled to write this ridiculous article.

# AWARD

THE ORDER OF THE BLUE TOAD is herewith awarded to Norman Cousins, editor of the *Saturday Review*, for putting out a boring, stupid magazine. His list of reviewers is enough to make anyone die of boredom—Granville Hicks, Doris Betts, Ben Ray Redman, Alma Lutz, Vincent Sheean, Lynn Montross, Stanley M. Swinton, *et al*. Why waste paper on such junk? The only good things the *Saturday Review* has published in the last five years were Schweitzer's atom-test appeal, and Ciardi's blast against Anne Morrow Lindbergh. However, someone soon quenched Ciardi's ardor; and his department has now settled down to the same level of mediocrity as the rest of the magazine.

The *Saturday Review* now has 'Quarterly Roundups' of poetry. There is something very funny about this. It is beginning to resemble a medical journal devoting its efforts to reviewing basketball games. Norman Cousins' efforts to prevent people from bending to the Atomic Energy Commission seem absurd when the magazine itself bends to every wind—it is eager to shift its whole format at the first breath from long-playing records, achievements in children's books, travel, stereophonics; what next? Therefore, we say that if Cousins wants to bore people to death and still get rich, he will have to accept insults. We therefore award him **The Blue Toad,** painted on a background of bedroom slippers, couched and rampant. The Toad is riding a fast turntable, and croaking scientific maxims.

# PAUL CELAN

M<small>R. C</small>ELAN WAS BORN IN 1920 IN A PART of Rumania, a section which he describes perhaps more accurately as a 'province of the old Hapsburg monarchy'. This area was of course occupied by the Germans during the war. It is said that some of his near family died in the German concentration camps; his poem on the camps, 'Death Fugue', moves with considerable conviction. It is also said that the poem was not liked very well by some German editors when it was written several years ago.

Most of what we know of Celan for certain comes from the short acceptance speech he gave in 1957 when he was given the Literature Prize of the Free City of Bremen. This speech was published in *Die Neue Rundschau*, First Issue, 1958, and we have translated parts of it here. He said that 'the landscape from which I come may be unknown to most of you, and it was a landscape in which the old Hassidic tales were at home, the same tales which Martin Buber has retold for us all in German.' There, he mentions, he first heard the name of Rudolf Alexander Schroeder, and Germany being then inaccessible, the only thing accessible was the German language, in which he began to write—to speak, to 'open up reality before me . . . it is related to the question of the meaning of the minute-hand.' 'For poetry is not timeless.'

Paul Celan's poems, though being obviously written for one time, are sunk deeply into an inward world, and in many ways they seem much stronger than the French surrealist poetry of twenty years ago, and in many ways represent an advance on them. The poems are more surrealistic in that the 'literal order of nature' is broken again and again with great confidence and at the same time the poetry seems more clear. They seem more deeply inward, for instance, than Breton's work. It is not poetry of direct statement, but of magnificent and rich images: 'We love one another like poppies and memory.' 'The poem, when it is a genuine manifestation of the language and thus in the nature of a talk . . . is like a bottle ready to come to shore. . . . It is the efforts of him who . . . is without protection in a sense not known about till recently, who takes his very life into speech.'

# MIRKO TUMA

Mirko Tuma was born in Czechoslovakia in 1920. When the Germans came he spent some years in a concentration camp, and his father died there. After the war, in the three 'interim' years, he published a great deal in Prague: he published several books of poems, several plays which were performed in the Prague theatres, and he was the editor of a critical monthly which presented articles on current plays, novels, and poetry, and new poems by young Czech poets.

A few weeks after the Russians took over the government, Mr. Tuma left Czechoslovakia, and went to London, where another Czech poet of this century, Ivan Blatny, is living, and also the Polish poet, Czeslaw Milosz. Mr. Tuma worked for the Voice of America in London for some time, and in 1954 came to work for the Voice of America in this country, and is now living in New York. Two of his new plays have recently been optioned for production here.

Mr. Tuma's poems show how closely Czechoslovakia was aligned to the culture of the rest of Europe, and especially Czech poetry to French poetry. The poetry is somehow very agile, and immensely resourceful. It is, without question, modern.

Besides the several books of poetry published in Prague, one book of poems by Mr. Tuma was published in New York in 1954 by The Friends of Czech Poetry, and the shorter poem translated here is taken from that volume. The longer poem is published here for the first time in both Czech and English. It was written to a visiting nurse in one of the large hospitals in New York, who one day, on meeting him in the hospital took a taxi home, and brought back the Pastoral Symphony of Beethoven and played it for him. As he says:

> The Pastoral Symphony
> like a river blossoming from the palms of a virgin
> dissolved the steel of the beds of hospitals
> and lightning clashes clustered on the branches
> of that lone tree

Mr. Tuma later wrote this poem, and dedicated it to her.

## AMERICAN CONTRIBUTORS

JAMES WRIGHT lives in Minneapolis. He has spent much time in recent months in translations of Georg Trakl and Cesar Vallejo, and we print here two of his recent poems.

MARGARET SCHEININ lives in Brooklyn Heights, one or two doors from where Hart Crane used to live. She writes that the site of his house is now a dormitory for Jehovah's Witnesses. This is the first poem she has published, except for poems in college periodicals. She was born in Columbus, Ohio.

JEROME ROTHENBERG is the originator of Hawk's Well Press. Readers who might like to read other poems of Celan will find them in the anthology Rothenberg has edited and translated, called *New Young German Poets*, to be published by Ferlingetti at City Lights soon.

GEORGE KRESENKY makes his living as the gardener of a fruit orchard on the Eastern shore of Lake Michigan. He graduated from Antioch College last year, and this is his first published poem, though two of his translations of the Spanish poet, Rafael Alberti, were recently published in Canada.

LOUIS SIMPSON's new book, *A Dream of Governors*, will be published by Wesleyan University Press in September in their new series of poets, just beginning. In the first issue of this magazine there was a short study of his work. He writes that he has spent the summer reading Spengler's *The Decline of the West*, in New York.

DAVID IGNATOW was born in Brooklyn, has never left New York for more than three months in his life, and he now runs a family business, The Enterprise Book Binding Co., Inc., in lower Manhattan. He admires the hard prose style of Hemingway, both for the depth it can evoke in common experiences, and for the diction, clear and suggestive at the same time. Mr. Ignatow has published two books of poetry, *Poems*, Decker Press, 1948, and *The Gentle Weight Lifter*, Morris Gallery, 1955.

DENISE LEVERTOV's new book *With Eyes at the Back of Our Heads* will be published by New Directions this fall. She has published one book in England, and two in America, which were *Here and Now*, published by City Lights in 1957, and *Overland to the Islands*, published by Jonathan Williams, Highlands, North Carolina, in a beautiful edition in 1958. She now lives in New York.

We have had many intelligent and interesting letters commenting on issues raised in the second number of *The Fifties*. In arguing that the poetry of the Black Mountain group is not avant-garde we do not claim that the poetry in *The Fifties* is; on the contrary, we believe there is no real avant-garde in American poetry. The term avant-garde or modernist movement, or new literature movement, has, we believe, an overlooked meaning: it has been used in Europe and South America for nearly a century to describe *poetry heavy with images from the unconscious*. In such art it is the unconscious, not the reason, which dominates. It is possible for poets to be familiar with French and Spanish verse, and yet not be influenced deeply by the most significant characteristic of French and Spanish poetry—the profound inner experience brought upward as imagery. Pound and Williams have consistently looked for a poetry of clarity and reason; the poets who have learned from them have accordingly aimed for a spare, bare poetry, and one result is a poetry of very few images. This neglect of the unconscious and absorption in reason we interpret to be the stamp not of modern French or Spanish movements, but of our own Emersonian or Puritan, American isolationist tradition. It is a great tradition, but it has dominated too long.